SAMUEL BARBER
Music for Organ

T0079940

ED 4441
Second Printing: June 2013

ISBN 978-1-4234-6542-3

G. SCHIRMER, Inc.

DISTRIBUTED BY

HAL•LEONARD®
CORPORATION

7777 W. BLUEMOUND RD. P.O. BOX 13819 MILWAUKEE, WI 53213

www.musicsalesclassical.com
www.halleonard.com

CONTENTS

Student Counterpoint Exercises

* First editions, previously unpublished

NOTES ON THE MUSIC

Previously Unpublished Works

Chorale for a New Organ

Composed for the new Kilgen organ at Westminster Presbyterian Church in West Chester, Pennsylvania on August 29, 1936. Premiered in 1936 by Westminster Presbyterian organist Ruth Thomas.[1] With twenty-three bars, *Chorale for a New Organ* is easily Barber's shortest organ work. It possesses a charming individuality and refreshing harmonic language, which adds another strain to Barber's flourishing earlier style, if only in miniature. *Chorale for a New Organ* can be easily performed on an instrument of just one manual.

Prelude and Fugue for Organ

Composed in 1927 during Barber's student days at the Curtis Institute of Music. While a student of Rosario Scalero he came into contact with Carl Weinrich, later Director of Music at Princeton University Chapel and an editor of many contemporary organ works. After showing the work to George Antheil in Vienna, *Prelude and Fugue for Organ* was premiered by Weinrich at Curtis on December 10, 1928.[3]

The prelude is written in the style of a trio. Indeed, the rhythmic ostinato figure in the pedals almost suggests a string trio, save for the expansive ranges of the manual parts. Marked *Andante, molto sostenuto*, the steady 3/4 quarter-note pulse in the pedal anchors a hauntingly beautiful duet above. As with the subsequent fugue, the manual range is quite large and requires at least a two-manual instrument in order to avoid a collision of hands. The prelude is largely written in the style of a tonal canon with brief alternating interludes that occasionally employ imitation. The chromatic harmony brings to mind the later organ works of Brahms and the more simply textured pieces of Reger.

The writing in the fugue is generally idiomatic for the instrument with the exception of some large stretches for the right hand of a thirteenth at bar 22 and elevenths at bars 24 and 54. These intervals present some obstacle to maintaining the legato touch this style of piece seems to engender. This can be accommodated by the early release of the upper voice in deference to the subject heard below. Registration markings were added to Barber's manuscript of the fugue by Scalero.[1] It is difficult to tell whether the registrations for the prelude came from Barber, Scalero, or Weinrich as they appear in different hands in the manuscript. However, irrespective of who notated or influenced the registration markings, the information provided allows the modern performer a glance towards the performance practice of the day. The registrations show that this piece is in a constant, if not symphonic, sense of aural transition and development.

To Longwood Gardens

In April 1925, Barber wrote his first organ work *To Longwood Gardens* and dedicated it to Mr. and Mrs. Pierre S. du Pont, as a thank you for the concerts he had attended at their home, Longwood Gardens. Along with a copy of the score, Barber sent a letter to Mr. du Pont in which he describes the piece, explaining that the work is constructed around the idea of a visitor entering Longwood, and the visitor's thoughts at the conservatory. He explains how the piece begins with a chorale akin to one written or improvised by the past organ masters. The visitor's thoughts wander in confusion when confronted with all the beauty of the garden, and Barber reflects this in the music that follows the chorale. Now calm and collected, the visitor listens to bird calls in the garden. At the conclusion of the work, Barber states that he paints a picture of the visitor leaving the garden, having found a new sense of peace.[2]

Firmen Swinnen first performed the piece at Longwood Gardens on May 10, 1925. Swinnen had been organist at Antwerp Cathedral until the outbreak of war, when he moved first to the UK and then ultimately to the US. He became organist at the Rialto Theatre in New York City and later the Rivoli Theater. In the age of the silent film, Swinnen was a noted exponent in the art of improvisation. The new Aeolian organ at Longwood would have been a special delight in this regard, with stops ranging from celestas and harp to a full range of orchestral colors.

While the nature of the house organ may seem extraordinary to the modern reader, it is worth noting that in the early twentieth century they were a regular feature in homes of the wealthy. For instance, in New York City the well-known names of Carnegie, Cartier, Gershwin, Romberg, Schwab, Tiffany, Vanderbilt, and Woolworth all had instruments installed in their residences, as did dozens of other prominent families.

Barber's Longwood letter, referenced above, helps us understand that this early but substantial work is an especially sectional one. That said, while not in any sense a symphonic poem, it is clearly a piece intended to be full of aural imagery that is replete with contrast and no leanness of creative spirit.

Barber's understanding of the instrument, as in later works, is well developed. All notes are clearly written within range and, with the rarest of exceptions, there is a keen understanding of organ technique. Although Barber did benefit from instruction in the organ, there is no evidence that it was lengthy or that a substantial amount of repertoire was studied. However, all the essential ingredients towards composition are found in this early piece. The only curious fact emerges in relation to Barber's hand-written comments, when he notes in the letter to du Pont that he has written the registrations in the score. The manuscript actually bears only minor suggestions for organ registration. The employment of the harp stop is specified as are the dynamics, but no more. This is in marked contrast, to the *Prelude and Fugue for Organ*, which was registered in some detail.

— Iain Quinn

Student Counterpoint Exercises

Manuscript sources: Library of Congress. All were apparently written as assignments in Barber's study of composition with Rosario Scalero at the Curtis Institute of Music. Scalero taught composition in a rigorously disciplined and traditional manner, requiring the mastery of counterpoint from various historical eras and all forms. Barber studied with Scalero for many formative years, from 1925 until 1934. Scalero was a cherished father figure for the young composer. Besides lessons at Curtis, Barber also resided with the Scalero family during several summers in Italy and continued studies there.

It is debatable whether these counterpoint exercises qualify as keyboard pieces. They look as such, notated on the grand staff, and could have been intended for organ, or could have been simply conceptual.

Partite Diverse sopra "Herr, straf mich nicht in deinem Zorn," Set I
According to Barber scholar Barbara Heyman, Barber composed these in September and October of 1926. In Barber's diary, documented by Heyman, on October 1, 1926 the composer wrote, "Mr. Scalero was wonderful to me – said my Chorales showed real promise but too homophonic. Starting six-part counterpoint and more chorales next week." [1] Barber may well have intended the set for organ.

Partite Diverse sopra "Herr, straf mich nicht in deinem Zorn," Set II
The manuscript is dated March 31, 1927. In Barber's diary, documented by scholar Barbara Heyman, his March 25, 1927 entry states, "I am going to get to work and write a real Chorale Partita now, so I can get on to the Fugue. I am getting tired of these boring chorale preludes." Then on March 31: "Wrote quite a good Chorale Partita and it was hard as the dickens to make myself to it." [1] It appears that Barber may have been writing specifically for organ, although the manuscript does not explicitly state as such.

— Richard Walters

Published Works

Adagio for Strings, Op. 11
Adagio for Strings originated as the second movement in Barber's String Quartet in B minor, Op. 11 (1936-38). The composer arranged the movement for string orchestra and it was premiered by Toscanini and the NBC Symphony Orchestra in New York City on a November 5, 1938 radio broadcast. In 1939, organist William Strickland met Barber in New York. At the time of their meeting, Strickland was assistant organist at St. Bartholomew's Church. He conducted an early performance of Barber's choral work *A Stopwatch and an Ordnance Map*, Op. 15 at the Army Music School in Fort Myers, Virginia, in 1942. At first uninterested when Strickland proposed an organ transcription of *Adagio*, Barber wrote him on August 15, 1945 and allowed the organ arrangement, which was published by G. Schirmer in 1949. [3]

Chorale Prelude on "Silent Night" from *Die Natali*, Op. 37
The orchestral work *Die Natali* was commissioned in 1954 by the Koussevitzky Music Foundation in conjunction with the Boston Symphony Orchestra. Busy at work on his opera *Vanessa*, it would take Barber six years to complete *Die Natali*. The full orchestra piece was premiered by Charles Münch and the Boston Symphony Orchestra on December 22, 1960 in Symphony Hall, Boston, Massachusetts. The work is comprised of themes stemming from Christmas carols, including "Silent Night." Barber particularly liked the variations on "Silent Night," and transcribed the *Chorale Prelude on "Silent Night"* for organ in 1961. [3]

Suite for Carillon
The carillon is a stationary set of large, chromatically tuned bells that are typically hung in a tower and played from a keyboard and pedal board. Between 1929-1933, the Curtis Institute of Music sent students to the Bok Singing Tower at the Mountain Lakes bird sanctuary in Lake Wales, Florida, to study carillon. The Bok Tower Gardens, on the estate of Edward and Mary Curtis Bok, were constructed in 1927. While at the Singing Tower, Barber took lessons from carillonneur Anton Brees and composed his *Suite for Carillon*. [3] The suite was commissioned by Edward Bok, husband of Mary Curtis Bok, founder of the Curtis Institute of Music. The first and fourth movements were performed by Anton Brees on the carillon at Bok Tower Gardens on April 4, 1931. [1] Subsequent movements were added, with the suite completed in 1932 and published in 1934. The suite has been included in this collection because it lends itself to performance on the organ.

Wondrous Love, Op. 34
Composed 1957-October 1958. [1] Commissioned by Christ Episcopal Church, Grosse Point, Michigan, for the inauguration of their new three-manual Walter Holtkamp organ. Dedicated to Richard Roeckelein, the organist of the church, and premiered by him there on October 19, 1958. Barber based his piece on the shape-note hymn "What wondrous love is this, oh! my soul!" The hymn was first published in William Walker's *Southern Harmony* in 1844, and reprinted in the earliest edition of *The Sacred Harp*, Atlanta, Georgia, in 1844. [1] Previously published, a facsimile of the shape-note hymn with S.M. Denson's 1911 added alto line has been retained and appears on page 36 of this collection.

— Joel K. Boyd

[1] Barbara Heyman, *A Comprehensive Thematic Catalog of the Works of Samuel Barber* (New York, NY: Oxford University Press, manuscript copy consulted prior to publication)

[2] Samuel Barber, Excerpt from a Letter to Mr. du Pont, 1925 (Hagley Museum and Library, Wilmington, DE)

[3] Barbara Heyman, *Samuel Barber: The Composer and His Music* (New York, NY: Oxford University Press, 1992)

Adagio for Strings

Pipe Organ

Great: 8'	Sw. to Ch.
Swell: 8', 4'	Sw. to Gt.
Choir: 8', 4'	Ch. to Gt.
Pedal: 16', 8'	Sw. to Ped.
	Ch. to Ped.

Hammond Organ

U	B♭ ⑩ 00 5676 542
L	B♭ ⑩ 00 2211 100
P	43

Samuel Barber, Op.11
Arranged for organ by
William Strickland

On all Models except E play 8va lower. On Model E disregard P 48, but couple Gt. to Pedal.

* See footnote on previous page.

Chorale for a New Organ

Samuel Barber
Edited by Iain Quinn

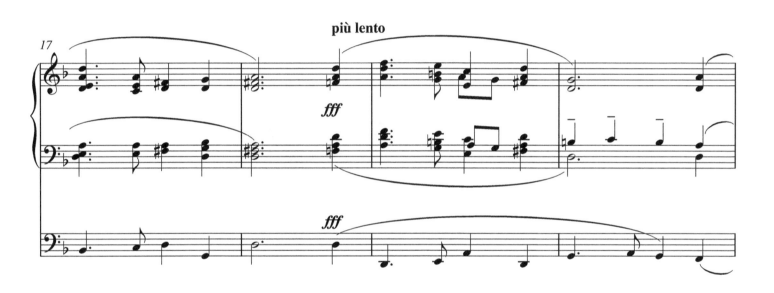

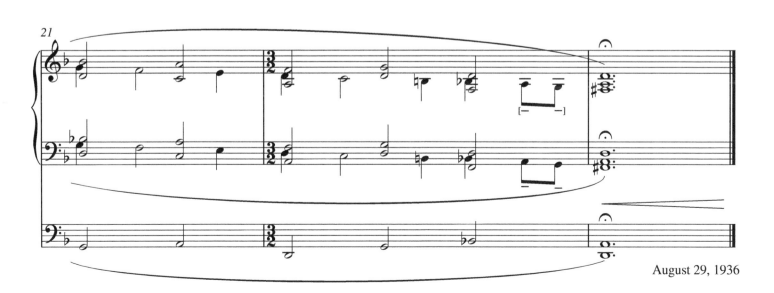

August 29, 1936

Chorale Prelude on "Silent Night"

from *Die Natali*, Op. 37

Samuel Barber
Transcribed for organ by the composer

Prelude and Fugue for Organ
Prelude

Samuel Barber
Edited by Iain Quinn

October 28, 1927

Fugue

(Great and Swell,) 8', 4'
Solo Strings
Choir Strings
Sw. to Gt., Gt. to Ped., (Sw. to Ped.)
Solo to Gt.

November, 1927

Suite for Carillon
I.

Samuel Barber

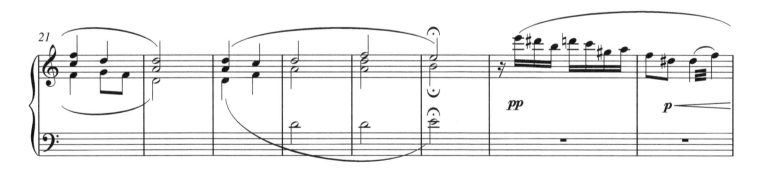

II. Scherzetto

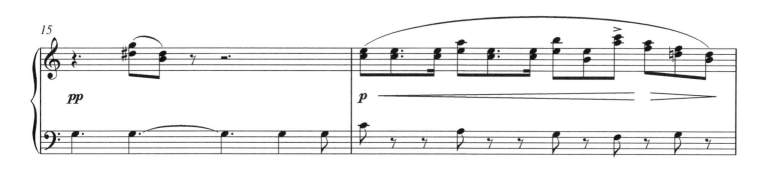

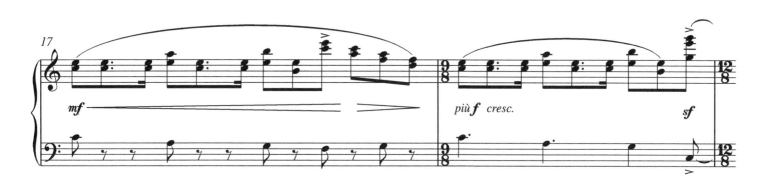

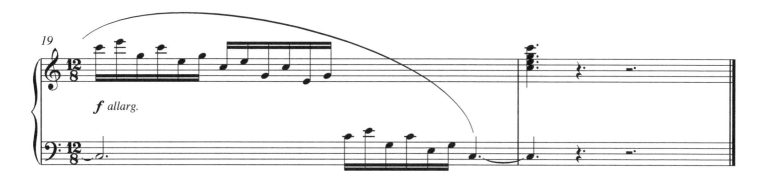

III.

Andante, un poco mosso

*C-natural published in 1934 Curtis Institute of Music/G. Schirmer edition, but confirmed as C-sharp in Heyman *A Comprehensive Thematic Catalog of the Works of Samuel Barber*, page 104.

IV. Finale

*All chords should be played with the fingers [when performed on the carillon].

To Mr. and Mrs. Pierre S. du Pont

To Longwood Gardens

Samuel Barber
Edited by Iain Quinn

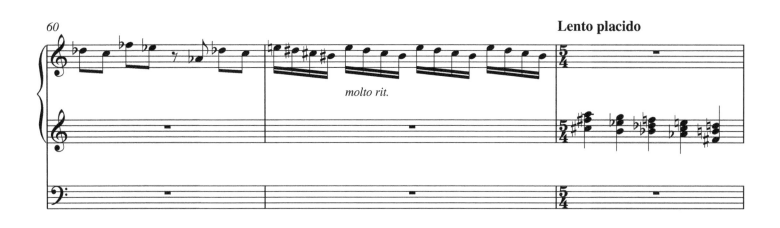

April, 1925

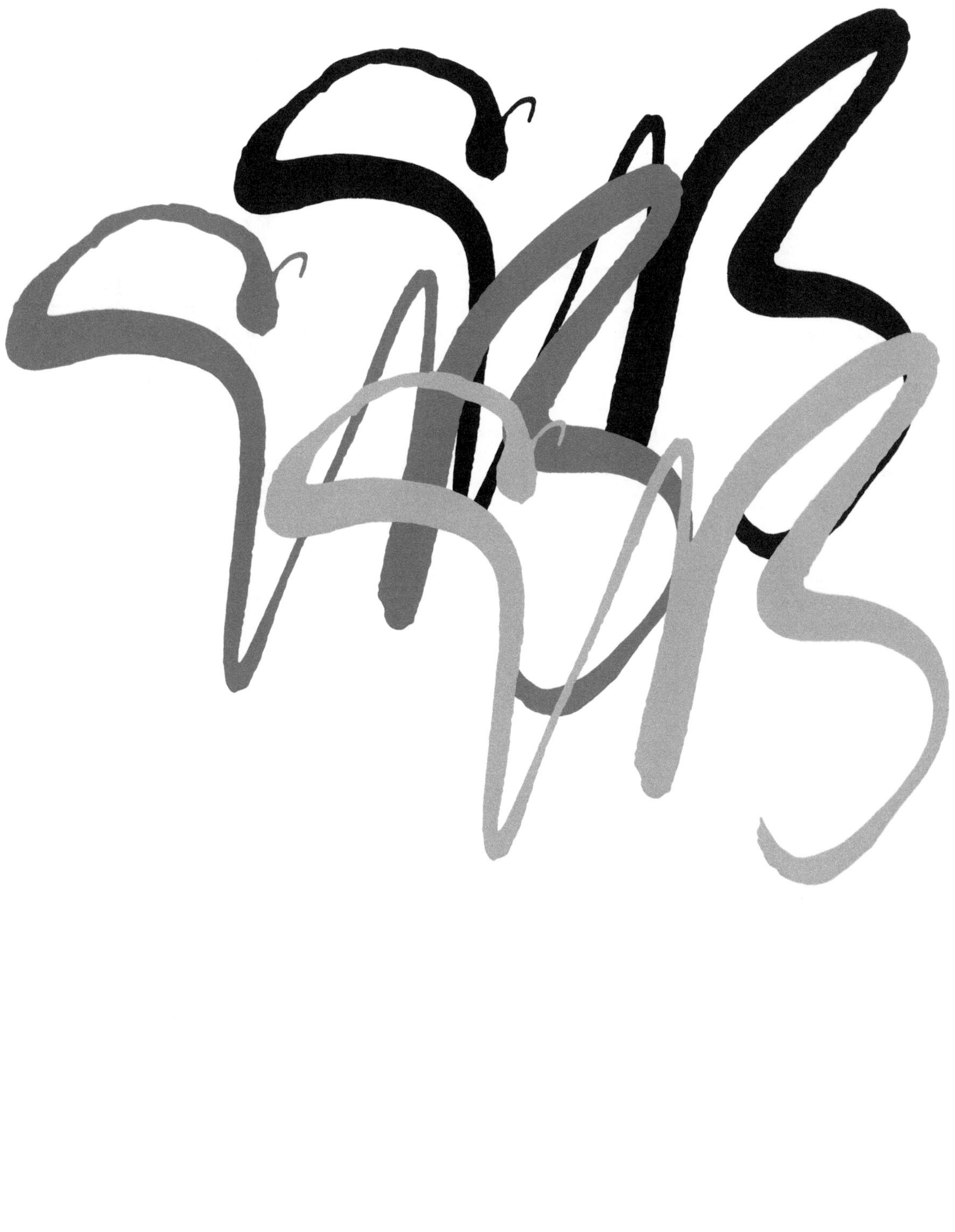

WONDROUS LOVE. 12, 9, 6, 6, 12, 9.

"For God so loved the world, that he gave his only begotten Son, that whosoever believeth in him, should not perish, but have everlasting life." — John 3:16.

Key of F minor.

Alto by S.M. Denson, 1911.

1. What wondrous love is this! oh, my soul! oh, my soul! What wondrous love is this! oh, my soul! What wondrous love is this

2. When I was sinking down, sink-ing down, sink-ing down, When I was sink-ing down, sink-ing down, When I was sink-ing down

3. To God and to the Lamb, I will sing, I will sing; To God and to the Lamb I will sing; To God and to the Lamb,

4. And when from death I'm free I'll sing on, I'll sing on, And when from death I'm free I'll sing on, And when from death I'm free

That caused the Lord of bliss To bear the dread-ful curse for my soul, for my soul, To bear the dread-ful curse for my soul.

Be - neath God's right-eous frown Christ laid a - side His crown for my soul, for my soul, Christ laid a - side His crown for my soul.

Who is the great I Am, While mil-lions join the theme, I will sing, I will sing, While mil-lions join the theme, I will sing.

I'll sing and joy - ful be, And thro' e - ter - ni - ty I'll sing on, I'll sing on, And thro' e - ter - ni - ty I'll sing on.

The authorship of the words and music of this tune are unknown. The words represent the great manifestation of the love of God for the world, in giving His only begotten Son to die for the world and that all who believe in him shall not perish but have everlasting life. No greater love has ever been expressed in the world than this. This tune is one of the stirring melodies of the old sacred songs and is yet loved and highly appreciated by the church people in many sections of the country. Tune was printed in the "Southern Harmony," 1835, page 282.

For Richard Roeckelein

Wondrous Love
Variations on a shape-note hymn

Sw.   8' Diap.
Gt.   Fl. 8' + 4'
Ch.   with light mixtures
Ped.   16' + 8' + Sw. to Ped.

Samuel Barber, Op. 34

* December 23, 1966 source lists the tempo variant *Same tempo.*

(Heyman *A Comprehensive Thematic Catalog of the Works of Samuel Barber,* page 276)

* mm. 79-80, December 23, 1966 source lists the tempo variant *Much slower. Molto espressivo*.

(Heyman *A Comprehensive Thematic Catalog of the Works of Samuel Barber,* page 276)

Partite Diverse sopra "Herr, straf mich nicht in deinem Zorn" Set I

I.

Samuel Barber
1926

II.

III.

IV.

Partite Diverse sopra "Herr, straf mich nicht in deinem Zorn" (Set II)

I.

Samuel Barber
1927

II.

III.

IV.

Canone alla quarta